CONTENTS

EXTRA RESOURCES/PERCUSSION	2	-	
CAST LIST	3	-	
SCRIPT and SONG LYRICS	4	-	
FULL NARRATION (with songs)	-	1	
SONGS (incl. percussion)			
Who's That Stealing My Lettuces?	10	2	7
Rapunzel, Let Your Hair Down	12	3	8
There Goes The Prince	14	4	9
Rapunzel's Song	17	5	10
Let's All Celebrate!	19	6	11
COPYRIGHT INFORMATION	24	-	

© 2010 Out of the Ark Ltd

Extra Resources

We have provided a number of extra resources to accompany this *'Song and Story'* book/CD. **To download the following, visit our website at www.outoftheark.com/resources**.

- Story/script in a child-friendly font so children can read as they listen to the narrated story *(CD track 1)*
- Mini-books with simplified story (for easy reading) and space to illustrate the story
- Lyric sheets

Percussion Notes

Percussion parts are included for all the songs *(see music score)* and we have also suggested areas in the script where percussion can be used for sound effects. Encouraging the children to play along with the songs will enrich their musical experience, helping with co-ordination and teamwork. Have fun including as much as you like and experiment with making other 'instruments' from everyday objects you might find at home or in the classroom.

Cast List

Main characters:

Narrator — Suitable for an adult/older child, or easily divided into shorter sections for a number of different children.

Wife — A small role at the beginning of the play with just one line.

Husband — No lines to say, but should be nimble on his feet and good at stealing lettuces!

Witch — Just a few short, simple lines to remember. Needs to have some confidence and an aptitude for being witchy!

Rapunzel — The leading role with the option of a solo in song 4. Just a few lines to remember, and a little acting ability would go down well. (Long hair not compulsory, but it would be handy.) *A doll is required for the scene where the husband and wife give their baby to the witch.*

Prince — Handsome and dashing – but if you're struggling to find that, a child with confidence and the ability to ride a hobby horse will do. A few short lines to remember.

Ideas for non-speaking parts:

In addition to the speaking parts in this musical, there are lots of opportunities to involve more children throughout the play. The main body of your performers can stand in the 'choir', with some playing percussion *(see Percussion Notes)*. They should all join in with the unison lines throughout the script and you could allocate others to set the scene:

The witch's garden — Children could be dressed as flowers and vegetables, swaying gently in the breeze. With a bit of imagination and artistic licence, they could also be picked by the husband and taken off to the wife.

The woods — Children dressed in appropriate colours could act as the trees in the wood. The prince can wind his way through them whilst galloping on his trusty steed, and Rapunzel can hide amongst them when banished from her tower.

Script and Song Lyrics

NARRATOR Once upon a time there was a man and his wife. At the back of their house was a little window where they could see a beautiful garden, full of wonderful flowers and vegetables. The garden had a high wall around it and no one dared to enter because it belonged to a fearsome old witch.

The wife longed to eat the lovely fresh salad vegetables that grew in the garden. She knew that she could not have them and as every day went by she got paler and thinner. She begged her husband to find a way into the garden to steal some of the vegetables.

WIFE I will get better if I have some of those salad vegetables.

NARRATOR So the man climbed the wall into the garden and he took some of the salad vegetables back to his wife. They were so delicious that she wanted to eat more of them. The next night her husband went back into the garden, but as he climbed down the wall, the old witch was waiting for him. She shouted at him in a very angry voice…

WITCH *(Angrily)* How dare you come into my garden?

Song 1. WHO'S THAT STEALING MY LETTUCES? CD track 2/7

1. Who's that stealing my lettuces?
   Who do you think you are?
   Who's that stealing my lettuces?
   You'll be sorry, ha, ha, ha!

2. Who's that stealing my radishes?
   Who do you think you are?
   Who's that stealing my radishes?
   You'll be sorry, ha, ha, ha!

3. Who's that stealing my spinach leaves?
   Who do you think you are?
   Who's that stealing my spinach leaves?
   You'll be sorry, ha, ha, ha!

4 Who's that stealing my cabbages?
Who do you think you are?
Who's that stealing my cabbages?
You'll be sorry, ha, ha, ha!

© 2010 Out of the Ark Ltd, Middlesex TW12 2HD
CCLI Song No. 5749564

NARRATOR The man was very frightened. He told the witch that the salad was the only thing that could make his wife well again. The witch thought for a while, then she told the man to take as much salad as he wanted. But the wicked witch wanted something in return.

WITCH You will give me your first-born child.

NARRATOR A year later, a baby girl was born and the witch came to take her away. She called the baby 'Rapunzel'.

When Rapunzel was 12 years old, the witch shut her up in a high tower in the woods so that she could never escape. It had one window right at the top and no stairs. Each day, the witch came to see Rapunzel. She stood at the bottom of the tower and shouted at the top of her voice…

WITCH (ALL) Rapunzel, Rapunzel, let down your hair!

NARRATOR Rapunzel threw her lovely plait of golden hair out of the window[1] and up climbed the witch.

Song 2. RAPUNZEL, LET YOUR HAIR DOWN CD track 3/8

1 Rapunzel, let your hair come tumbling down,
Tumbling down, tumbling down.
Rapunzel, let your hair come tumbling down
To the ground, down to the ground.

2 I'll hold on very tight and up I will climb,
Up I will climb, up I will climb.
I'll hold on very tight and up I will climb
To the top, top of the tower.

3 And through the little window, ever so small,
Ever so small, ever so small.
And through the little window, ever so small,
I will crawl, in I will crawl.

---

1 **Added percussion:** Slide a soft beater down a glockenspiel each time the hair falls down.

4 *Repeat verse 1*

© 2010 Out of the Ark Ltd, Middlesex TW12 2HD
CCLI Song No. 5749571

NARRATOR One day when the sun was shining and the birds were singing, a handsome prince came riding into the woods.[2] He rode as fast as lightning, galloping and galloping through the trees, on a big black horse.

Song 3.   THERE GOES THE PRINCE   CD track 4/9

1 Riding like the wind,
Like the wind, like the wind,
There goes the prince, there goes the prince.
Riding like the wind,
Like the wind, like the wind,
Galloping on, galloping on,
Galloping along.

2 Racing to the woods,
To the woods, to the woods,
There goes the prince, there goes the prince.
Racing to the woods,
To the woods, to the woods,
Galloping on, galloping on,
Galloping along.

3 Dashing through the trees,
Through the trees, through the trees,
There goes the prince, there goes the prince.
Dashing through the trees,
Through the trees, through the trees,
Galloping on, galloping on,
Galloping along.

4 *Repeat verse 1*

© 2010 Out of the Ark Ltd, Middlesex TW12 2HD
CCLI Song No. 5749588

NARRATOR The prince saw the tower in the distance and slowed down. As he passed the tower he could hear someone singing. He thought that it sounded very beautiful.

---

[2] **Added percussion:** Use good-old coconut shells for the horse's hooves.

Song 4. RAPUNZEL'S SONG CD track 5/10

Ideally, this song should be sung as a solo, with the bracketed lyrics (echo) sung by all.

Sing, sing, sing a song,
All day long, *(all day long)*.
Sing, sing, sing a song,
All day long, *(all day long)*.

© 2010 Out of the Ark Ltd, Middlesex TW12 2HD
CCLI Song No. 5749605

NARRATOR The prince waited behind a tree and listened to the singing for a long time. Day after day he returned to hear it. Then one day as he waited, the old witch appeared. The prince watched as she shouted out…

WITCH (ALL) Rapunzel, Rapunzel, let down your hair!

NARRATOR The prince couldn't believe his eyes as the old witch climbed up Rapunzel's hair and in through the window of the tower.

The next day, when the prince came back to the tower he heard the beautiful singing again.

Song 4. RAPUNZEL'S SONG CD track 5/10

Lyrics as above.

NARRATOR The prince stood underneath the tower, looked up at the little window and called out…

PRINCE (ALL) Rapunzel, Rapunzel, let down your hair!

NARRATOR The beautiful plait of hair fell to the ground and the prince climbed up. When Rapunzel saw him she was frightened, but the prince was very kind to her.

PRINCE I think you sing beautifully.

NARRATOR Rapunzel thought that the prince was wonderful and very handsome. As they talked, they fell in love and the prince asked Rapunzel to marry him. She was overjoyed and together they made a plan for Rapunzel to escape. Each day when the prince visited, he brought some silk which Rapunzel wove into a ladder.

	One day when the witch visited the tower, Rapunzel, without thinking, asked the witch…
RAPUNZEL	Why are you heavier than the prince?
NARRATOR	The witch was very angry. She got a big pair of scissors and in one snip[3] she cut off Rapunzel's hair. She took Rapunzel deep into the woods and left her there. Then she returned to the tower to wait for the prince. She didn't have to wait very long.
PRINCE (ALL)	Rapunzel, Rapunzel, let down your hair.
NARRATOR	The witch fastened the golden plait of hair to a hook, then threw it down to the prince. As the prince climbed through the window, there stood the angry old witch.
WITCH	You will never see Rapunzel again!
NARRATOR	In despair, the prince jumped from the tower. He fell among a patch of thorns which scratched his eyes and made him blind. The prince stumbled into the woods and wandered sadly along. He walked and walked for many days until finally he could not walk any more. The poor, blind prince sat down in despair among the leaves. But as he sat, not knowing what to do, he heard a sound in the distance. It was the sound of beautiful singing.

Song 4.　RAPUNZEL'S SONG　　　　　　　　CD track 5/10

Lyrics as on page 7.

NARRATOR	The prince could not believe his ears. It was his Rapunzel. Rapunzel saw her prince and ran towards him. As she cried with happiness, two tears dropped on to his eyes[4] and immediately the prince could see again.
	The prince took Rapunzel to his father's castle where they had a grand wedding. They lived happily ever after and the old witch was never seen again.

---

3 **Added percussion:** Use claves tapped together to create the snip sound.
4 **Added percussion:** Use 2 taps on finger cymbals or a triangle to symbolise the tear drops falling.

Song 5.   LET'S ALL CELEBRATE! CD track 6/11

1. Celebrations, celebrations,
   Let's all celebrate.
   Have you got your invitations?
   Meet us at the castle gate.

2. Jubilations, jubilations,
   Having a lovely time.
   Tell your friends and all relations,
   Tell them that it's turned out fine.

3. Celebrations, celebrations,
   Let's all celebrate.
   Have you got your invitations?
   Meet us at the castle gate.

© 2010 Out of the Ark Ltd, Middlesex TW12 2HD
CCLI Song No. 5749595

THE END

Who's That Stealing My Lettuces?

Words and Music by
Niki Davies

With a swing ♩ = 146

use a different percussion sound for each verse

xylophone

1. Who's that steal-ing my let-tu-ces?__ Who do you think you
2. Who's that steal-ing my ra-dish-es?__ Who do you think you
3. Who's that steal-ing my spi-nach leaves? Who do you think you
4. Who's that steal-ing my cab-ba-ges?__ Who do you think you

© 2010 Out of the Ark Ltd, Middlesex TW12 2HD
CCLI Song No. 5749564

are? Who's that stealing my lettuces?
are? Who's that stealing my radishes?
are? Who's that stealing my spinach leaves?
are? Who's that stealing my cabbages?

You'll be sorry, ha, ha, ha! ha, ha, ha!
You'll be sorry, ha, ha, ha!
You'll be sorry, ha, ha, ha!
You'll be sorry,

Rapunzel, Let Your Hair Down

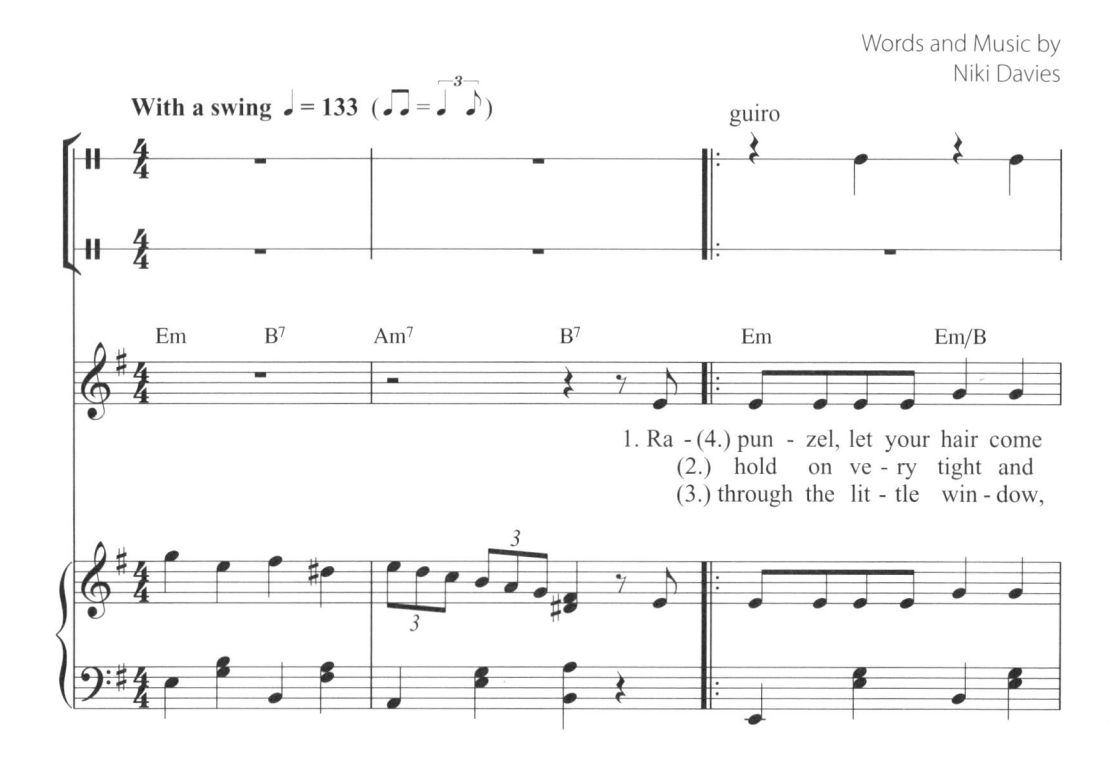

Words and Music by
Niki Davies

With a swing ♩ = 133

1. Ra - pun - zel, let your hair come tum - bl - ing down, tum - bl - ing down, tum - bl - ing down. Ra-
(2.) hold on ve - ry tight and up I will climb, up I will climb, up I will climb. I'll
(3.) through the lit - tle win - dow, ev - er so small, ev - er so small, ev - er so small. And

© 2010 Out of the Ark Ltd, Middlesex TW12 2HD
CCLI Song No. 5749571

-pun - zel, let your hair come tum-bl - ing down to the ground,____ down to the ground.__
hold on ve - ry tight and up I will climb to the top,____ top of the tower.__
through the lit - tle win - dow, ev - er so small, I will crawl,____ in I will crawl.__

triangle

(+ wind chimes ad lib.)

2. I'll
3. And
4. Ra -

There Goes The Prince

Words and Music by
Niki Davies

With energy ♩. = 120

1. 4. Ri - ding like the wind, like the wind, like the wind, there goes the prince, there goes the
2. Ra - cing to the woods, to the woods, to the woods, there goes the prince, there goes the
3. Dash - ing through the trees, through the trees, through the trees, there goes the prince, there goes the

© 2010 Out of the Ark Ltd, Middlesex TW12 2HD
CCLI Song No. 5749588

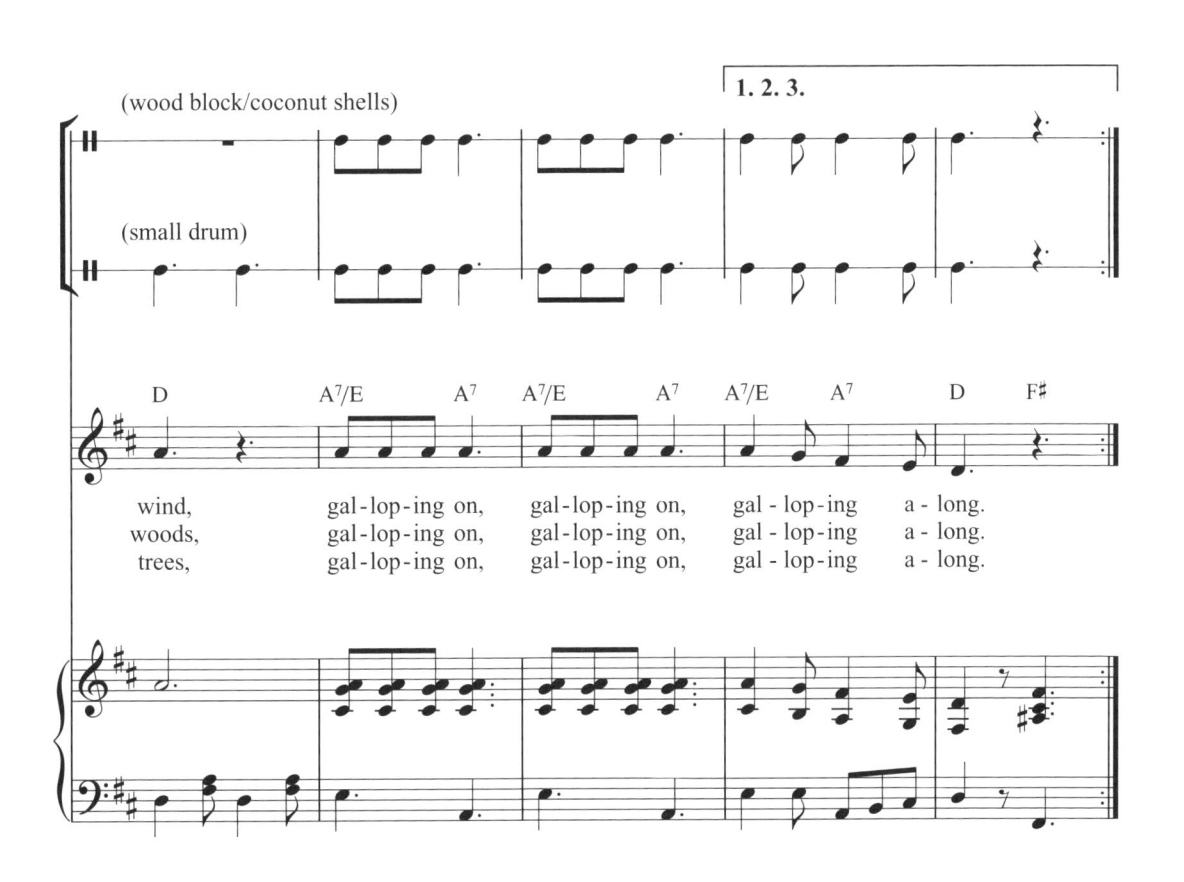

prince. Ri - ding like the wind, like the wind, like the
prince. Ra - cing to the woods, to the woods, to the
prince. Dash - ing through the trees, through the trees, through the

(wood block/coconut shells)

(small drum)

1. 2. 3.

wind, gal-lop-ing on, gal-lop-ing on, gal-lop-ing a - long.
woods, gal-lop-ing on, gal-lop-ing on, gal-lop-ing a - long.
trees, gal-lop-ing on, gal-lop-ing on, gal-lop-ing a - long.

gal - lop-ing   a - long.

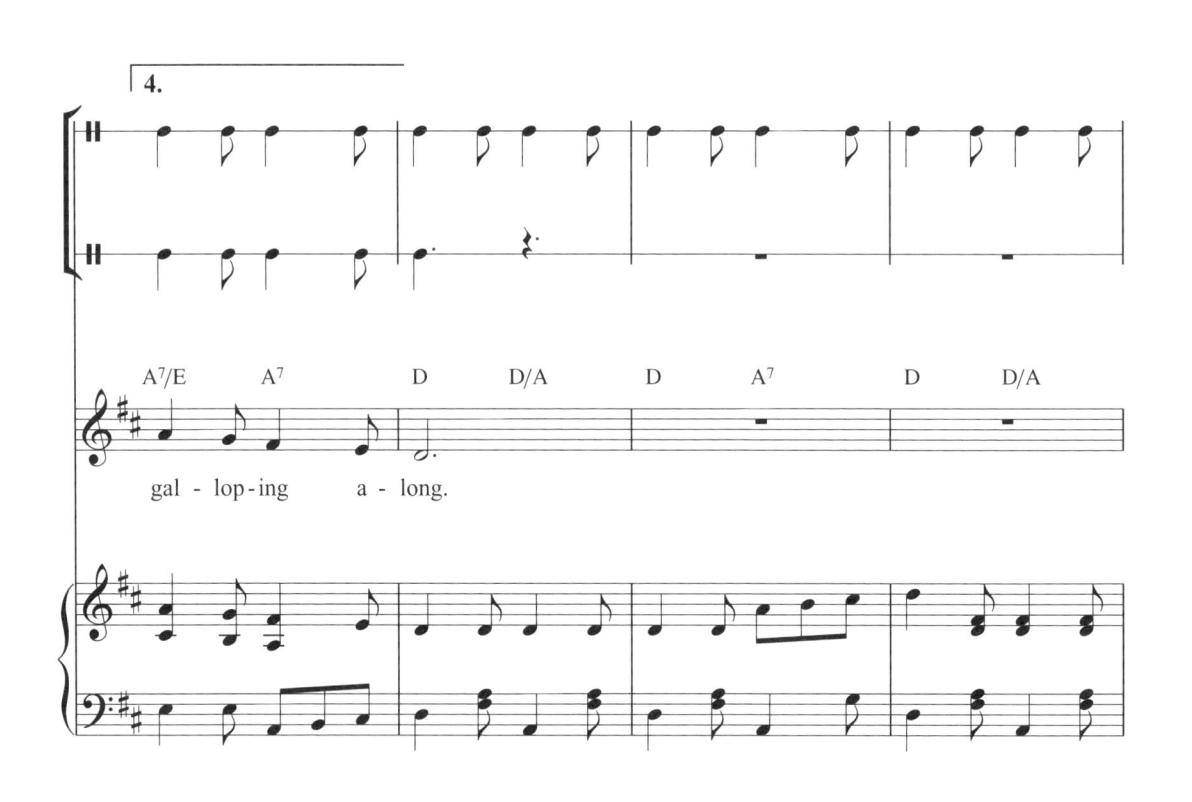

Rapunzel's Song

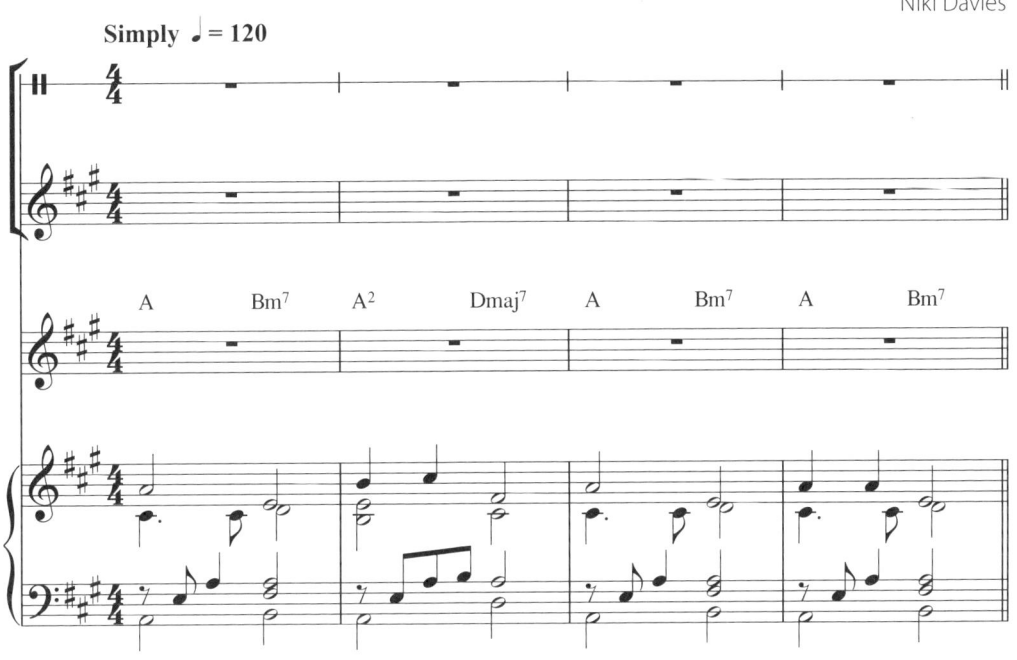

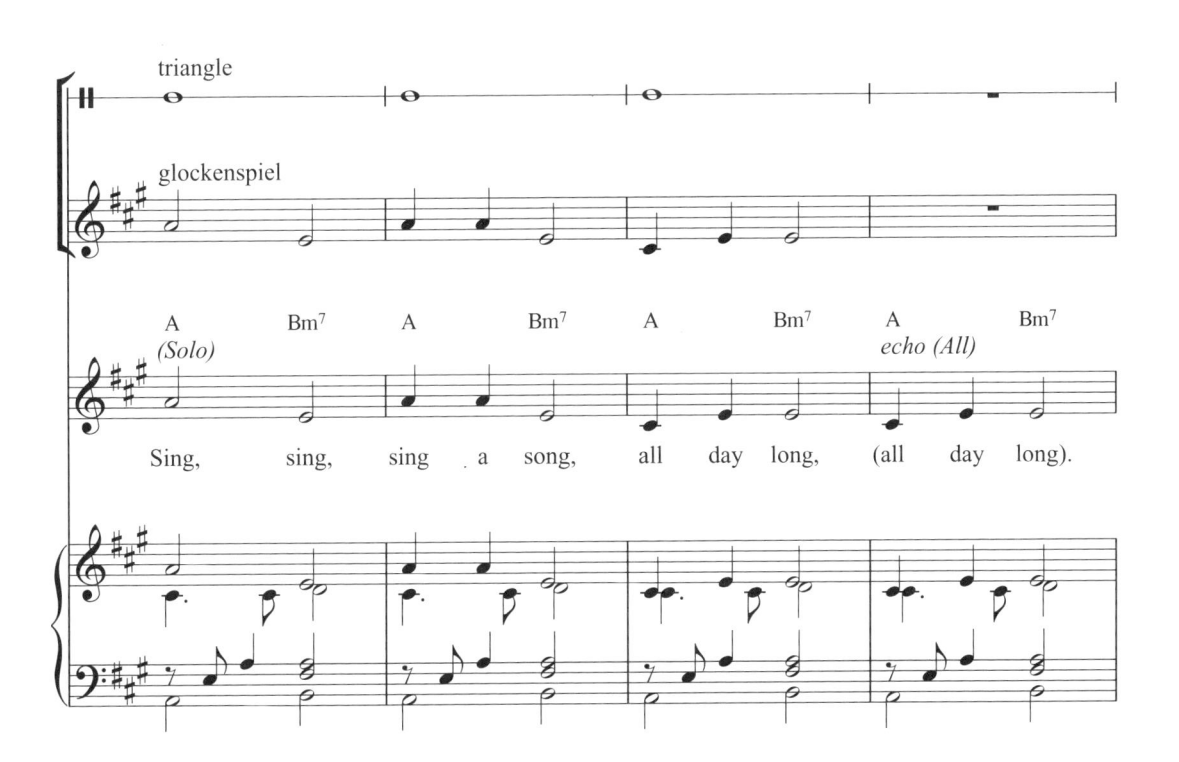

Words and Music by
Niki Davies

Simply ♩ = 120

triangle

glockenspiel

(Solo)   echo (All)

Sing, sing, sing a song, all day long, (all day long).

© 2010 Out of the Ark Ltd, Middlesex TW12 2HD
CCLI Song No. 5749605

Sing, sing, sing a song, all day long, (all day long).

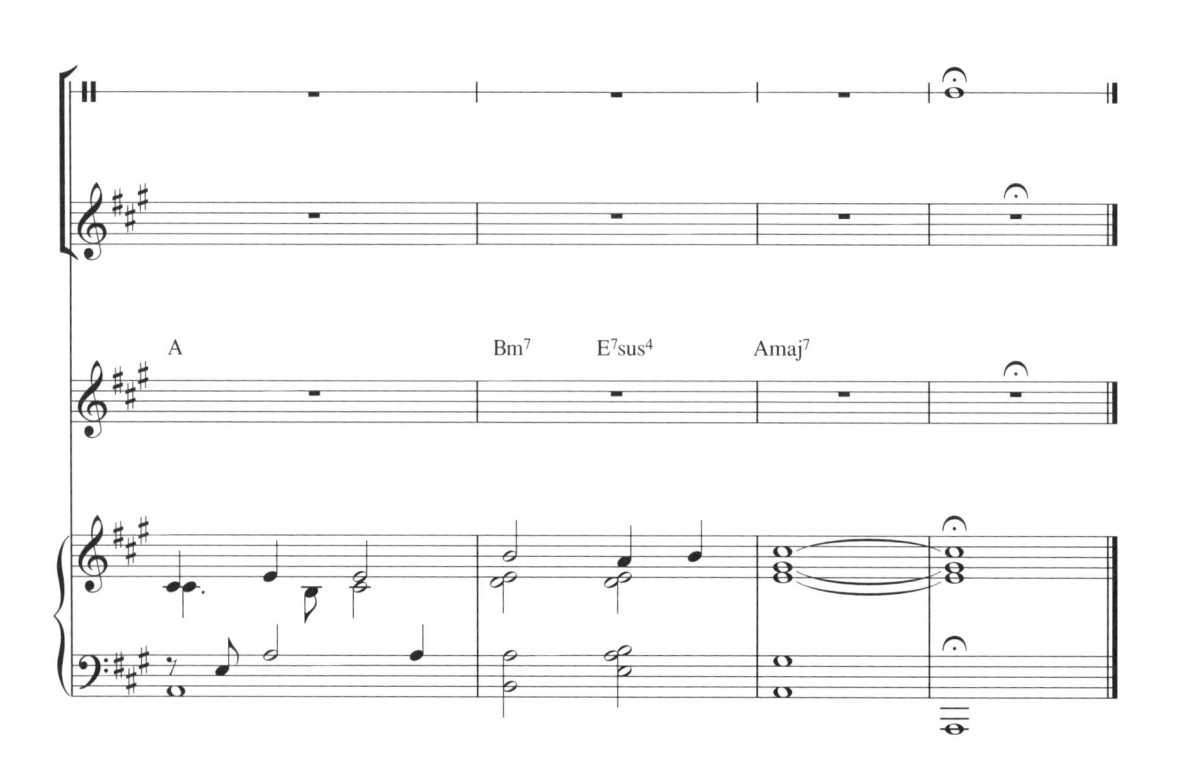

Let's All Celebrate!

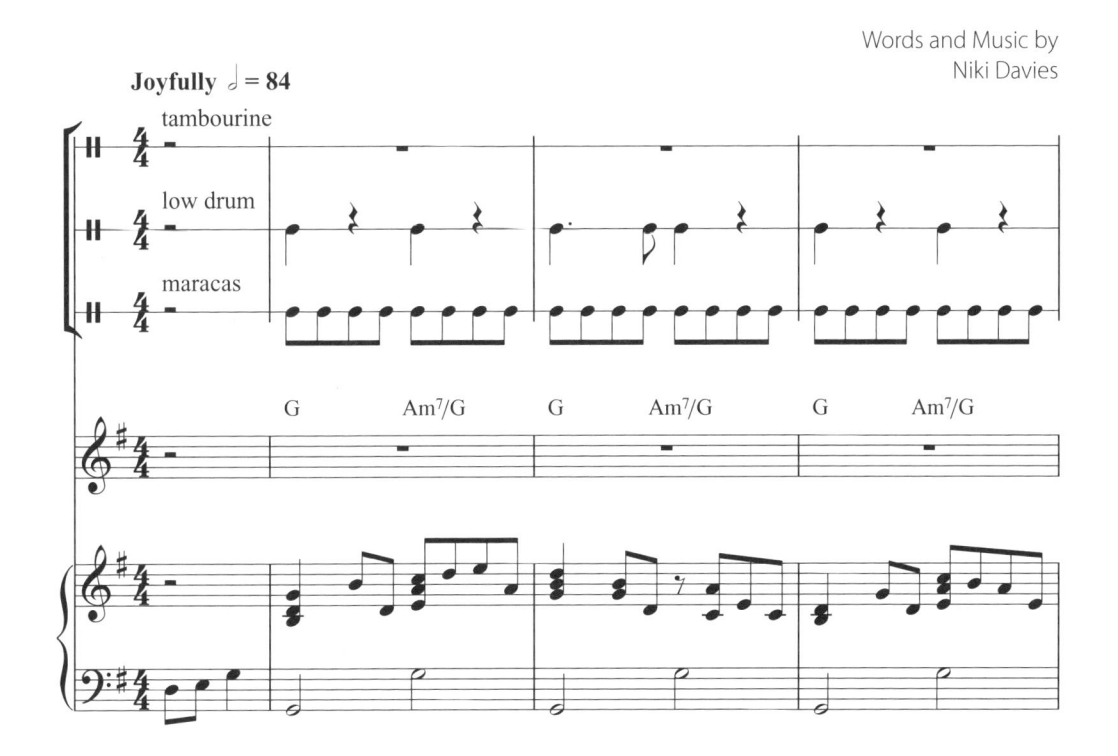

Words and Music by
Niki Davies

1.3. Ce - le - bra - tions, ce - le - bra - tions,
2. Ju - bi - la - tions, ju - bi - la - tions,

© 2010 Out of the Ark Ltd, Middlesex TW12 2HD
CCLI Song No. 5749595

let's all ce - le - brate. Have you got your in - vi - ta - tions?
hav-ing a love - ly time. Tell your friends and all re - la - tions,

To Coda ⊕ **1.**

Meet us at the cas - tle gate.
tell them that it's turned out

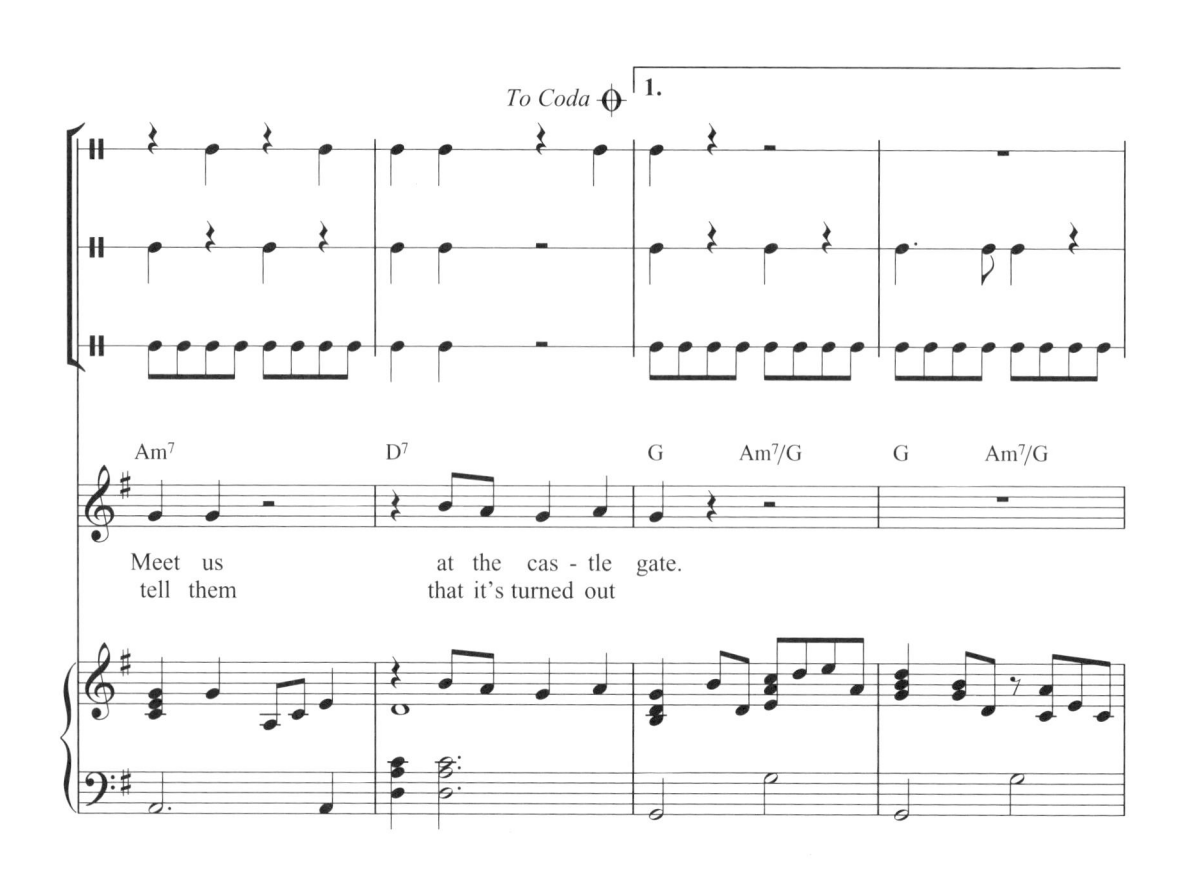

21

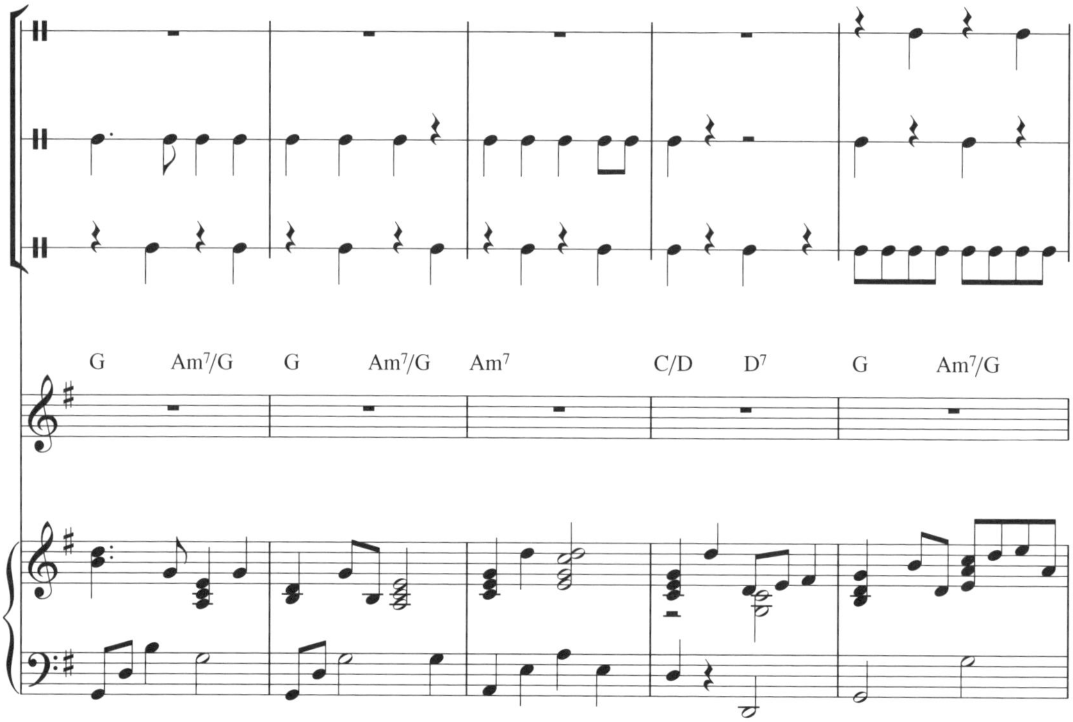
G
Am7/G
G
Am7/G
Am7
C/D
D7
G
Am7/G

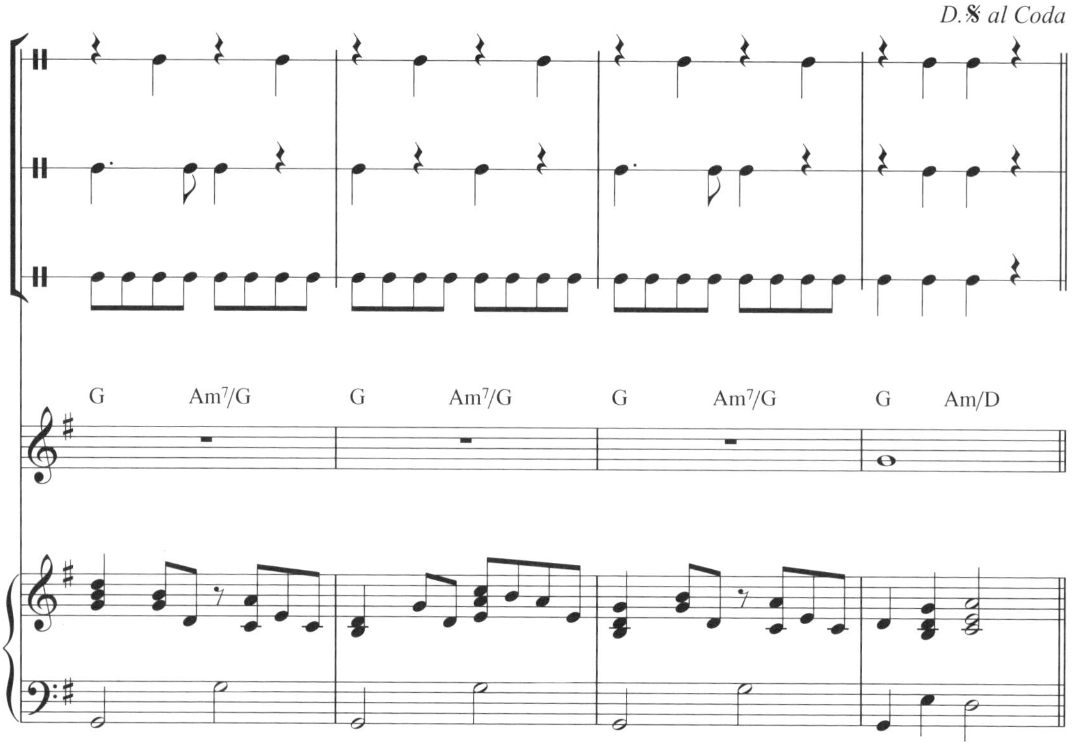
D.𝄋 al Coda
G
Am7/G
G
Am7/G
G
Am7/G
G
Am/D

CODA

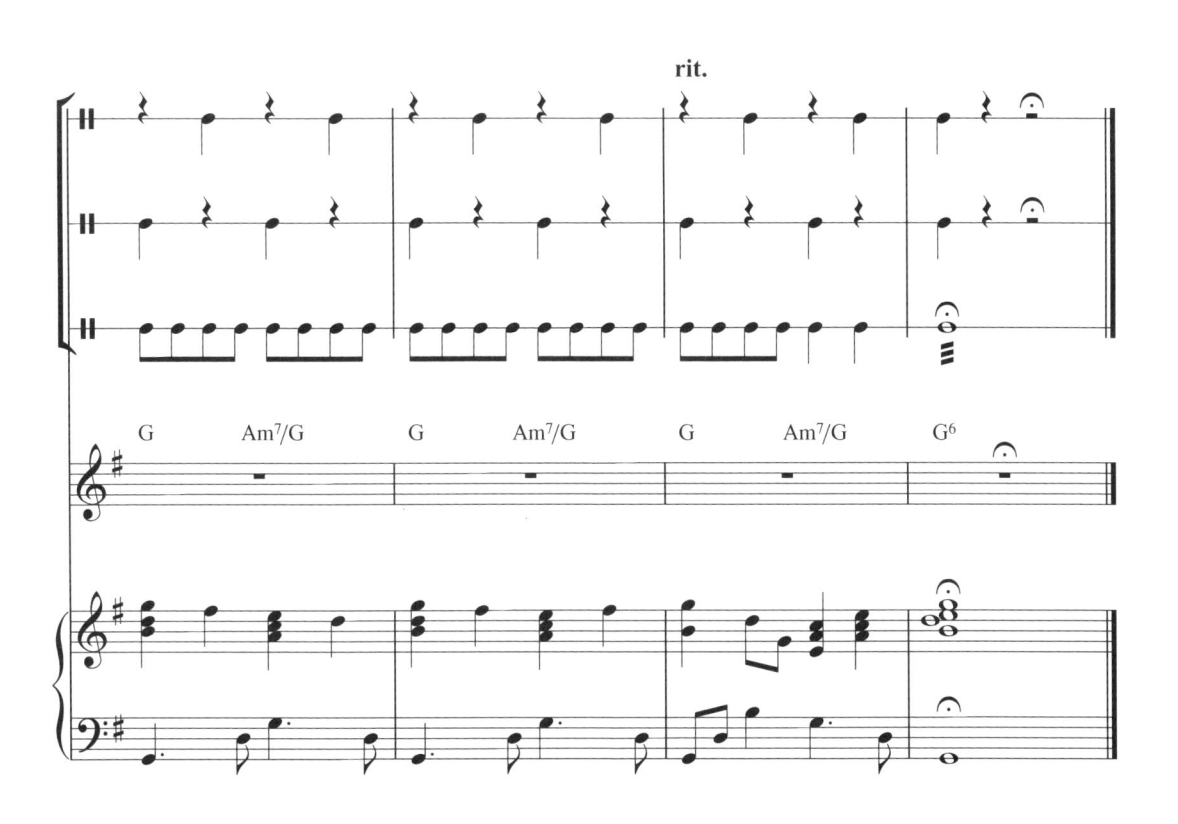

gate.

rit.

Copyright & Licensing

VERY IMPORTANT

You are free to use the material in our musicals for all teaching purposes. However, the performance of musicals or songs to an audience and the reproduction of scripts, lyrics and music scores are subject to licensing requirements by law. A licence has been granted for certain performances within the purchase price of this book and CD package – see below for details.

Helpful information about licensing can also be found on the following website:

'A Guide to Licensing Copyright in Schools' www.licensing-copyright.org

And remember, we're happy to help. For advice contact our customer services team:

UK: 020 8481 7200   International: +44 20 8481 7200   copyright@outoftheark.com

---

(1) Performance of Musicals

The performance of a work involving drama, movement, narrative or dialogue such as a musical requires a specific licence from the publisher. **Your PRS licence does not cover musicals.**

If your school is performing *'Rapunzel'* by Niki Davies as a musical on school premises, to an audience of staff, pupils and their families, then to simplify the process we have already granted an inclusive licence giving permission to stage such a performance.

If you are performing *'Rapunzel'* for any other type of audience please contact Out of the Ark Music directly to apply for a performance licence.

(2) Licensing of Audio and Video Recordings

Copying Out of the Ark Music's audio CDs is not permitted without obtaining a licence from the publisher. File-sharing or installation of Out of the Ark Music's audio CD tracks on to a computer are strictly forbidden. To make an audio or video recording please contact Out of the Ark Music directly.

(3) Other use of the published material

If you are not staging a musical but still intend to use material from the publication then different licences are required:

(a) Reproduction of Song Lyrics or Musical Scores

The following licences from Christian Copyright Licensing Ltd (www.ccli.com) permit photocopying or reproduction of song lyrics and music scores, for example to create song-sheets, overhead transparencies or to use any electronic display medium.

For UK schools: 'Collective Worship Copyright Licence' and 'Music Reproduction Licence.'
For churches: 'Church Copyright and Music Reproduction Licence.'

Please ensure that you log the songs that are used on your copy report. (Organisations that do not hold one of the above licences should contact Out of the Ark Music directly for permission.)

(b) Performance of Songs

If you are not staging a musical but are performing any of our songs for the public on school premises (ie for anybody other than staff and pupils) then royalty payments become due. Most schools have an arrangement with the Performing Rights Society (PRS) through their local authority. Organisations that do not have such an arrangement should contact Out of the Ark Music directly.